EASY
Word Games

Building Language Skills through Rhymes,
Hink Pinks, Rebus Riddles, and More

BY JO FURR

SCHOLASTIC
PROFESSIONAL BOOKS

New York • Toronto • London • Auckland • Sydney

Dedication

To Dr. Lee Mountain, my teacher and friend, who helped me stretch my wings and fly.

Acknowledgments

Having fun with words all started more than 35 years ago when I met my husband, Jim Furr. His propensity for puns and verbal humor convinced me early on that I'd better join 'em or leave 'em. My daughter, Erin, and son, O'Neal, carry on the legacy of punning, and I thank you all for your patience and encouragement.

Thank you, Susan Boepple, for sharing your enthusiasm and creativity with me during our years of teaching first grade together at West University Elementary. Susan created the "sillies" game on page 46. Thanks to Martha Low and Brenda Stabell, my second grade teaching partners at St. John's school, for enduring patience and support.

I'd like to thank my students at St. John's School: Sallie Armstrong, Sarah Bryan, Patton Bushong, Alexander Crain, John Crain, Katherine Donnelly, Jim Elkins, Hannah Fogler, Andrew Gagel, Rachel Hiller, Julia Kahn, Diana Kirkland, Rebecca Linn, Sean McNeely, Will Nelson, David Noel, Sarah Noel, Jonathan Payne, Stephen Spencer, Wesley Stedman.

A special thank-you goes to Helen Sorvillo of Scholastic Professional Books.

"Catch a Little Rhyme" from *Catch a Little Rhyme* by Eve Merriam. Copyright © 1966 by Eve Merriam. Used by permission of Marian Reiner for the estate of the author.

"I love Words" by Eva Grant from *Instructor* Magazine. Copyright © 1976 by Scholastic, Inc. Reprinted by permission of publisher.

Cover design by Vincent Ceci and Jaime Lucero
Interior design by Drew Hires
Illustrations by Drew Hires

ISBN 0-590-67475-7
Copyright © 1996 by Jo Furr
Printed in the U.S.A.

12 11 10 9 8 7 6 5 4 3 2 1   6 7 8/9

Table of Contents

Introduction

Why Use Wordplay in the Classroom?

As teachers, we want to instill in our students a love of language, reading, and writing. And, as often as possible, we want to make learning fun. Word games provide an easy and natural way to accomplish these goals.

I've found that incorporating wordplay into my day-to-day classroom activities really does enhance children's acquisition of literacy. Playing and interacting with words helps students recognize sound-letter relationships, connect words with ideas, understand word usage, identify word families, develop spelling skills, and expand their vocabulary. All of this helps prepare them for encountering rich language in their reading. Likewise, it's a means of enriching their own writing. Using word games, riddles, and picture puzzles is also an excellent way to get kids to focus their attention, think critically and creatively, and problem-solve.

Integrating Word Games into Your Curriculum

I don't teach a specific unit on wordplay at one point in time. Instead, I try to infuse word play into all areas of the curriculum, and that's the approach I hope *Easy Word Games* will help you to take.

This book offers some simple ways to play with language. It includes games you can use anytime, and with little prior planning. Whether you like activities that students can complete more or less independently, or you prefer to work closely with your students on in-class activities, you'll find you can adapt the games, reproducible activities, and manipulatives to suit your style.

Ways to Use the Activities in This Book

Here are some suggestions for using the activities in this book in your classroom:

❥ **Learning Centers:** Learning centers need to contain lots of materials for students to choose from, in order to reinforce the skills being taught. Many of the activities in this book are ideal for this purpose. Once students are familiar with word games, you can place baskets of reproducibles and manipulatives, and some of the suggested books, in a wordplay learning center. For more ideas on using learning centers to enrich language and literacy, see *Learning Centers: Getting Them Started, Keeping Them Going,* by Michael F. Opitz, Scholastic Professional Books, New York, 1995, or *Quick and Easy Learning Centers: Word Play* by Mary Beth Spann, Scholastic Professional Books, New York, 1995.

❥ **Morning Brain Teasers:** Children love a challenging routine for independently beginning each school-day morning. My students come in, say good morning to each other, and take care of chores like putting backpacks away, signing in for lunch, placing homework in the "Homework" basket, and getting their supplies ready. Then, the fun really begins! I write a brain teaser on the chalkboard or pass out a reproducible. These brain teasers can include any type of problem-solving, critical-thinking, or language-rich puzzle, and they prompt even the most reluctant starter to get going.

There are two easy methods of presenting these brain teasers. Some mornings I introduce children to a type of wordplay, then write a sample of that wordplay activity on a 16" x 24" spiral chart and stand it on the chalk ledge all day. I invite children to solve the brain teaser in their notebook or journal. We discuss the solution at the end of the day or first thing the next morning. Sometimes I simply leave copies of a word game in a basket in a central room location. Children pick up a copy and solve it during the day, for discussion later, or they may leave it in a basket for me to check. Rebuses (see pages 52-55) are especially good for morning brain teasers.

❥ **Listening Activities:** I may read a problem or group of problems orally, for a listening activity. Children write down their answers and put them in a box to be read later in the day. Riddles in particular work well as listening activities. (See pages 19-23 and 26-27 for hink pink and homonym-riddle activities.)

❥ **Time Fillers:** Even in the most well-organized classroom, emergencies can arise, opening up a block of time for which you haven't planned an activity. The games in this book require minimal planning and materials, yet they exercise thinking skills. Have copies of a game on hand to distribute when a time gap opens. Also, in classes grouped heterogeneously, there may be a few students who always seem to finish assignments before everyone else, only to wonder what to do next. Having a store of these fun word games readily available can solve that problem.

❥ **Take Homes:** Word games are a great way to involve families in students' learning. Distribute copies of a reproducible page and model in class how to solve the first problem on the page. Invite students to take the page home to complete with family members. Family members may want to send in their own favorite word games or examples of wordplay they encounter in their reading at home.

Ideas for Displaying Word Games

As kids become acquainted with different word forms and instances of wordplay, you'll find that they begin recognizing examples of wordplay everywhere. I encourage kids to keep an eye—and an ear—out for wordplay. They may discover a new homonym in a book, hear alliteration in a playground chant, discover an anagram in a spelling word, and so on. In the classroom, I provide lots of places and ways for kids to record what they see and hear and to give them an opportunity for spontaneous play. You may want to try some of these display ideas in your own classroom:

❧ Bulletin Boards and Beyond: Designate an area in your classroom as a "Wordplay Place." Set up a table with baskets of books related to word play (see resource lists after each lesson). Tack up a bulletin board next to it where kids can display wordplay they discover on their own. Keep pencils, markers, crayons, scissors, and glue sticks on the table to facilitate kids' recording of wordplay they hear, see, or read. As an alternative to the bulletin board display, you could simply place a three-ringed binder filled with blank notebook paper on the table in which children can record instances of wordplay they come across. I allow children to quietly go over and record things in the binder any time they want.

❧ Hang-Ups: Keep a basket of sentence strips near the chalkboard, as well as clothespins and magnets. You and children can write examples of wordplay on the strips, then use the clothespins to hang the strips from the chalk ledge or magnets to hang them on the chalkboard.

❧ A Tree Full of Words: A small table tree (a bare tree branch stuck in a can full of pebbles for support works fine) provides a place for an ever-changing wordplay display. Write words on paper leaves or other seasonal shapes and hang them from the branches. (See the "Pick a Pair of Pears" activity on page 25 for ideas on how to use this tree.)

❥ Jot-on-a-Chart: Colorful, construction paper charts (12" x 18") hanging on cabinet doors, chalk boards, or walls invite writers to jot down all sorts of words and wordplay. Just tape up one sheet of construction paper at a time. Students can add to the charts as they discover wordplay any time during the day. As the sheets are filled, take them down and bind them together with large rings for class books. My students help come up with titles such as "Happy Homonyms," "Super Synonyms," "Delightful Describing Words," "Awesome Antonyms," and so on.

❥ Journals and Writing Notebooks: I invite each student to keep a three-ringed binder filled with loose-leaf notebook paper in his or her desk (or cubby or bin) in which to jot down any word play he or she reads or hears. This provides an opportunity for children to write spontaneously and privately as they learn about different aspects of our language. From time to time, students share entries from their journals with me and the rest of the class.

Words, Wonderful Words

Sharing the excitement, fun, and beauty of our language can become a natural part of every school day. I find that word games keep the classroom language-rich, and I consistently try to listen for, talk about, and model "playing" with language. The more materials you make available for spontaneous participation, discussion, and interaction, the more kids "think" language.

Be sure to invite them to create their own word games, logic puzzles, riddles, etc., to share with you, one another, and family members. I keep a basket on my desk in which students place any word games they create, and I often write their ideas on class charts. They feel quite honored when their game is used!

I hope you'll find word games and language activities in this book that suit your individual teaching style, as well as your students' needs. And, above all, I hope they enable you and your students to have fun with language.

Enjoy!

Chapter I

Playing with Sound

Alliteration

What's Alliteration?
Alliteration is the repetition of the same beginning sound in consecutive words or words in close proximity to each other.

Introducing Alliteration to Kids
Young children use alliteration quite naturally in their play. You hear it in jump-rope rhymes and playground chants and songs. After defining alliteration, invite children to recite any rhymes, chants, and songs they know that include allit- eration. Another fun way to intro- duce alliteration to kids is to have them play with tongue twisters. Invite students to try saying the ones from the list below three times fast. Be sure to invite kids to share their own favorites, too.

Examples to Share
Here are some tongue twisters that use alliteration:
- ☛ A skunk sat on a stump—the skunk thought the stump stunk, the stump throught the skunk stunk.
- ☛ A big black bug bit a big black bear and made the big black bear bleed blood.
- ☛ Famous Floyd Fudd Flingle flipped floppy, flat flapjacks.
- ☛ Sheep shouldn't sleep in a shack, sheep should sleep in a shed.
- ☛ Sly Sam slurped Sally's soup.
- ☛ Moose noshing much mush.

Ways to Play
❥ **Invent a Twister:** After kids practice the tongue twisters above, they might like to write their own. Ask each child to pick a different letter of the alphabet and use that letter to create a silly alliterative phrase or sentence. (If you have more than 26 children in your class, start over again with *a* at the 27th child. You may wish to eliminate difficult letters like *q, x,* and *z,* or you can partner up with the child who would have that letter before beginning play.)

Challenge kids to try to repeat interior consonant sounds as well, to make the twisters even harder to say. Reproducible page 11 includes a pattern kids can use to make "talking heads" on which to display their tongue twisters. To assemble the pattern, follow these steps:

1. Make an enlarged photocopy (25%-50%) of the pattern page for each child.

2. Tell children to cut out the patterns, then write their tongue twisters on the tongue part of the mouthpiece.

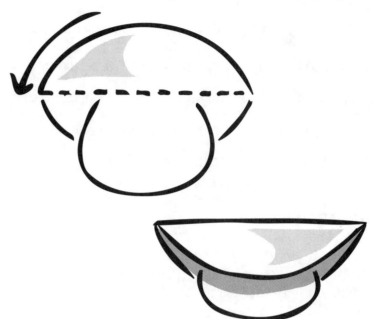

3. Have students fold and crease the mouthpiece in half, as shown.

4. Glue mouth to lower half of face, aligning edges of circles.

5. Students can use markers, glued-on yarn, and other craft materials to decorate their "talking heads" to resemble themselves.

6. Tack the "talking heads" to a bulletin board for an interactive display. Children can lift the mouthpiece flaps for some alliterative fun.

♦ **Alphabet Zoo:** Here's a fun game for kids to play orally: Assign each child a letter of the alphabet. (Again, you may have to assign more than one child to a letter; you may also want to skip the letters *q*, *x*, and *z*, or partner up with children assigned these letters.) Then write the following sentence fragment on the chalkboard:

"I had a . . ."

Ask children to take turns repeating the sentence fragment and adding the name of an animal that begins with their assigned letter. They must also include an adjective describing the animal that begins with the same letter. Children should proceed in alphabetical order. Model a few sentences with them before beginning play, to make sure students have the hang of this game. For example:

☞ "I had an awful alligator."

☞ "I had a big bear."

☞ "I had a curious crocodile."

☞ "I had a dirty dingo."

And so on.

Students may want to follow up this speaking activity by painting a mural of their "alphabet zoo" or by making an animal alphabet book (see resource list on the following page for alphabet books to use as models).

❥ **Write On:** As an alternate follow-up to the "alphabet zoo" activity, invite children to give their animals alliterative names and write alliterative stories about them. Children can compile and illustrate their stories to make a classroom anthology of alliterative animal tales. Share the example below with children to use as models in their writing. It was written by Will, one of my second grade students:

> . . . Alvy, my awful alligator ate a group of Australian archaeologists as they all ambled along. I yelled at him again and again, "Alvy, alright already!" Alvy didn't listen to me as I argued and said they would be angry, and want to be avenged, as well. He said, "AAAAhhhhh! I can't help it if I've got an alligator's appetite!"

Alliteration Resources

A Is for Angry: An Animal Adjective Alphabet by S. Boynton (Workman, 1987).

Alligators All Around: An Alphabet by M. Sendak (HarperCollins, 1962).

A My Name Is Alice by J. Bayer (Dial, 1984).

Animalia by G. Base (Abrams, 1987).

Animals Should Definitely Not Act Like People by J. Barret (Macmillan, 1980).

Aster Aardvark's Alphabet Adventures by S. Kellogg (Morrow, 1987).

C Is for Curious by W. Hubbard (Chronicle, 1990).

Great Gorilla Grins: An Abundance of Animal Alliteration by B. Hilgartner (Little, Brown, 1979).

Oh Say Can You Say? by Dr. Seuss (Random House, 1979).

17 Kings and 42 Elephants by M. Mahy (Dial, 1987).

A Twister of Twists, a Tangler of Tongues by A. Schwartz (HarperCollins, 1972).

The Z was Zapped by C. Van Allsburg (Houghton Mifflin, 1987).

Talking Head Pattern

Onomatopoeia

What's Onomatopoeia?
Onomatopoeia is the use of a word—like "buzz," "boom," "bang," or "clang"—that sounds like the noise it represents.

Introducing Onomatopoeia to Kids
For a cacophonic introduction to sound words, read aloud Eve Merriam's book *Bam Bam Bam*, which describes all the noises heard at a construction site. (Check out Merriam's poetry as well, which is rich in onomatopoeic language). Follow up the reading by dividing the class into groups, and asking the groups to brainstorm sound words related to other situations and environments, for example, onomatopoeia at the zoo (hiss, squawk, roar), in the cafeteria (crinkle, crunch, slurp), in the city (honk, screech, beep), in a rainstorm (whoosh, pitter-patter, kaboom), at a parade (ratta-tat-tat, crash, toot), and so on. Allow time for children to share their word lists.

Examples to Share

ah-choo	clang	crash
boom	kersplat	gurgle
slurp	cuckoo	moo
buzz	roar	tweet
chirp	twitter	creak
squeak	screech	plop
beep	crunch	swish
thump	bang	crackle
pop	ding-dong	zing
	ding-a-ling	

Ways to Play

❥ **Noisy Words:** Distribute a copy of reproducible page 14 to each child. In this cut-and-paste activity, students match the sound word with the person, animal, or object that makes it. For a fun follow-up, allow children to make noises and name onomatopoeic words that match the sound. Children can work in pairs, with one partner making the sound (by blowing a party horn, crashing cymbals, dropping a book on the floor, and so on) and the other labeling it. Encourage children to make up new onomatopoeic words if they can't come up with ones that exist already.

❥ **A Listening Walk:** Take your class on a walk through a sound-rich environment, such as a playground or city street. Be sure children come equipped with notebooks in which they can record the sounds they hear and the onomatopoeic words that represent some of those sounds. Back in class, each child can pick a sound; draw a picture of the person, animal, or thing that made it; label the sound; and use it as an entry in a class book entitled "Our Listening Walk."

❥ **Comics Corner:** Comics strips are famous for their use of onomatopoeia. Ask students to keep an eye out for sound words in comics, highlight them, and use them to create a bulletin board display. Invite children to draw comics of their own that are rich in onomatopoeia.

Onomatopoeia Resources

Bam Bam Bam by E. Merriam (Henry Holt, 1995).
Click, Rumble, Roar: Poems About Machines compiled by L. B. Hopkins (Harper Collins, 1987).
Horton Hears a Who by Dr. Seuss (Random House, 1954).

Name _____

Noisy Words

What sounds do these things make? Cut out the word strips below.
Then paste each sound word in the right speech balloon.

squeak	whack	tick-tick-tick
beep-beep	crash	ratta-tat-tat

Rhyme

What's Rhyme?

Rhyme is the pairing or stringing together of words that end with the same or similar sounds, lending a musical quality to poetry and other forms of writing and speaking.

Introducing Rhyme to Kids

Children should already be well acquainted with rhyme from their reading and other language arts activities. Pocket charts are a useful tool for playing with rhyme, since they allow children to manipulate rhyming words. To set up a pocket-chart activity focusing on rhyme, write the lines of a simple rhyming poem on sentence strips. Omit the second rhyming word in each pair of rhyming lines. Write these words on separate pieces of paper. Put the sentence strips in a pocket chart or tack them to a bulletin board. Place the separate rhyming words underneath the poem. Allow children to take turns finding the right place in the poem to insert each rhyming word.

Any short rhyming poem will work for this pocket-chart activity, but you may want to use the one below, which focuses on rhyme itself. Encourage students to come up with alternate rhymes to use in the poem.

Example to Share

I Love Words

Rhyming words:
Singing birds,
Soft blue sky,
Lullaby,
Lion's roar
Cellar door,
Blinking,
Winking,
Twinkling,
Sprinkling,
Dance with glee,
Melody,
Spun and sun!
Rhyming's fun.

— Eva Grant

Ways to Play

❥ **Get Ready to Rhyme:** Distribute a copy of page 17 to students to give them more time to play with rhyme. After students have filled in the blanks to complete the poem "Catch a Little Rhyme," encourage them to create new couplets to extend the poem—for example, "I put it in my hat, but it turned into a bat," and so on. Students can illustrate their couplets, as well as those in the original poem, and make an action-adventure book about rhyme.

❥ **A Rhyme in Time:** Here's a quick and easy spinner game children can play to gain practice in rhyming:

Setting Up the Game:

1. Children can play the game in pairs or small teams with equal numbers.
2. Provide each team with a copy of page 18 as well as oak tag, glue, scissors, a brass fastener, and a paper clip. Students should follow the directions on that page to make the spinner.
3. Teams will need pencils, paper, and a watch with a second hand, an egg timer, or an hourglass to keep track of time.

To Play:

1. Have teams take turns spinning. They must try to come up with as many rhymes as they can for whatever word the spinner lands on, in a pre-determined amount of time (1-5 minutes, depending on your students). The other team can keep track of time.
2. Teams take turns playing. If one team spins the same word that they or the other team has spun before, they get two more tries to spin a new word. If they fail to spin a new word, they give up their turn.
3. Teams get one point for every rhyme. The winner is the team with the most points after a set number of rounds of play (3-5, depending on students). Before students begin playing, allow teams to decide whether or not near rhymes (such as time and nine) will be counted.

Rhyme Resources

Building Literacy with Interactive Charts by K. Schlosser and V. Phillips (Scholastic Professional Books, 1995).
James Marshall's Mother Goose by J. Marshall (Farrar, Strauss, Giroux, 1979).
Thematic Poems, Songs, and Fingerplays by M. Goldish (Scholastic Professional Books, 1993).
The Random House Book of Poetry for Children compiled by J. Prelutsky (Random House, 1983).

Name _____

Get Ready to Rhyme

Pick a word from the box to make each pair of lines in the poem rhyme.
The first one is done for you.

skyscraper	door	whale	sight
rhyme	goat	cat	icicle

Catch a Little Rhyme

Once upon a time
I caught a little _____ rhyme _____

I set it on the floor
but it ran right out the _____

I chased it on my bicycle
but it melted to an _____

I scooped it up in my hat
but it turned into a _____

I caught it by the tail
but it stretched into a _____

I followed it in a boat
but it changed into a _____

When I fed it tin and paper
it became a tall _____

Then it grew into a kite
and flew far out of _____

— *Eve Merriam*

More! Make up a new pair of rhyming lines to add to the poem.
Write them on the back of this paper.

A Rhyme in Time

Follow these directions to make the spinner for the "A Rhyme in Time" game.

What you need:
- ◆ spinner pattern
- ◆ oak tag (8" x 10")
- ◆ glue
- ◆ scissors
- ◆ brass fastener
- ◆ paper clip

What you do:
1. Glue this pattern page onto the oak tag.
2. Cut out the spinner pattern.
3. Open a paper clip to form an *S* shape.
4. Use a brass fastener to attach one end of the open paper clip to the center of the spinner, as shown.

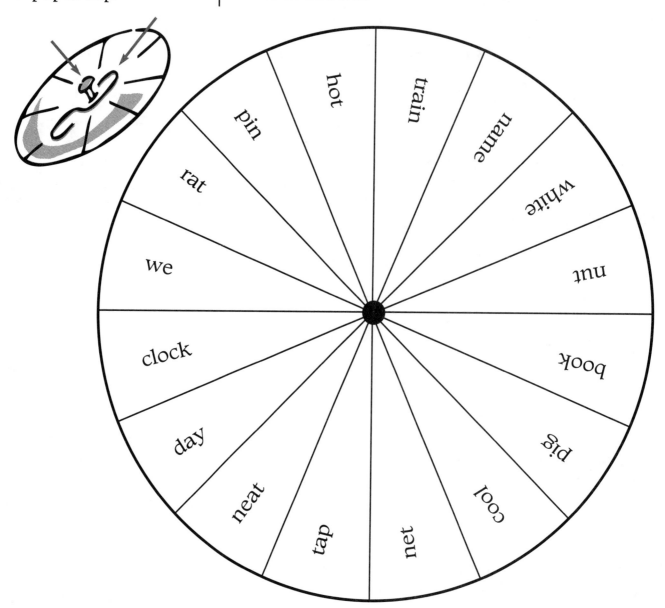

Hink Pinks, Hinky Pinkies, and Hinkity Pinkities

What's a Hink Pink?

A hink pink is another way to play with rhyme. It's a riddle in which the answer is a pair of rhyming words. In a hink pink, each of the words in the answer is a single syllable (just like the words "hink pink"). Hinky pinkies and hinkity pinkities are two variations on this riddle game. With hinky pinkies, the answer is always a pair of two-syllable rhyming words. With hinkity pinkities, the answer is a pair of three-syllable rhyming words.

Introducing Hink Pinks to Kids

The Hink Pink Book or What Do You Call a Magician's Extra Bunny? by Marilyn Burns is a great resource for acquainting kids with these riddle rhymes. As you move through the book, encourage kids to distinguish among the hink pinks, hinky pinkies, and hinkity pinkities by clapping out the syllables in the answers. If this book is unavailable, or if you want to give students more practice with hink pinks, you can share some of the examples from the lists below. Hinkity pinkities may prove too challenging for young children, but you may want to try a few with them anyway, just for fun.

What's a plate for tuna?

fish dish

Examples to Share

Hink Pinks

What's a plate for tuna? *(fish dish)*
What's something terrific to sit on? *(neat seat)*
What's something that you sip that's a pale red color? *(pink drink)*
What's a friendly squeeze from an insect? *(bug hug)*
What's a chilly place where people learn? *(cool school)*
What's a small, stinging insect? *(wee bee)*

Hinky Pinkies

What's a beautiful cat? *(pretty kitty)*
What's a skinny horse *(bony pony)*
What's a robin that talks too much? *(wordy birdie)*
What are scary flashes in a thunderstorm? *(frightening lightning)*
Who's someone who likes to eat saltines between meals? *(cracker snacker)*

Hinkity Pinkities
What's a frozen two-wheeler? *(icicle bicycle)*
What is faithfulness to a queen or king? *(royalty loyalty)*
What is a terrific rubber band *(fantastic elastic)*
What are noodles that aren't quite cooked? *(unready spaghetti)*

Ways to Play

❧ **Ready, Set, Rhyme:** After you've tried some hink pinks as a class, pass out reproducible page 21 and let kids try to solve some on their own. If you feel your students need more guidance, divide them into teams, read the hink pinks aloud, and let them brainstorm with classmates to try to solve the riddles. As an alternate oral exercise, provide students with the two-word rhyming answer, and ask them to come up with the question. Hink Pinks are as much fun to make as they are to solve. Encourage kids to come up with their own.

❧ **Animal Hink Pinks and Hinky Pinkies:**
Pages 22-23 contain a pattern for a flap book of animal hink pinks and hinky pinkies. To make the book:
1. Make a double-sided photocopy of pages 22-23, being careful not to invert the copy.
2. Provide each child with a copy of the page.
3. Fold in along the dashed line.
4. Cut flaps along the solid lines.

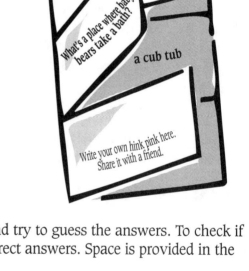

Kids can read the riddles on the front of the book and try to guess the answers. To check if they're right, they can lift the flaps to reveal the correct answers. Space is provided in the book for kids to write their own animal hink pink.

Hink Pink Resources

The Hink Pink Book or What Do You Call a Magician's Extra Bunny?
by M. Burns (Little, Brown, 1981).
One Sun by B. MacMillan (Scholastic, 1990).
Teaching Kids to Spell by J. R. Gentry and J. Gillet (Heinemann, 1993).

Name _____

Ready, Set, Rhyme

Can you solve the hink pinks and hinky pinkies on this page?
Draw a line to match the riddle with the answer.

What's an angry father?   **lazy daisy**

What's a flower that doesn't
want to work?   **June tune**

What's something on the stove   **loud crowd**
that you shouldn't touch?

                                                             damp lamp
What's a song sung in the summer?

                                                             mad dad
What's a wet light?

What's a noisy group of people?   **hot pot**

More! Here are three hink pinks: bear chair, nap cap, big pig. On the back
of this paper, write a question to go with each answer.

Animal Hink Pinks and Hinky Pinkies

What's a dinner party
for all the animals
in the zoo?

a beast feast

What's a chubby kitty?

What's a baby bird
with a cold?

What's a rabbit that
tells jokes?

What's a place where baby
bears take a bath?

_____

Write your own hink pink here.
Share it with a friend.
(Write the answer under the flap.)

Animal Hink Pinks and Hinky Pinkies

a fat cat

a sick chick

a funny bunny

a cub tub

_____

Chapter 2

Playing with Sense

Homonyms

What's a Homonym?

A homonym is a word that sounds the same as another word yet has a different meaning. It may be spelled the same or differently. (Note: When working with young children I use this general definition of homonyms. With older children, you might want to distinguish between homophones and homographs. Homophones are words that are pronounced the same, but may be spelled differently; homographs are words that are spelled the same, but may be pronounced differently.)

Introducing Homonyms to Kids

A fun way to acquaint children with homonyms is to read aloud parts of Lewis Carroll's *Alice in Wonderland*, which is replete with wordplay (including homonyms, idioms, puns, riddles, and rhyme). At one point in the book, for example, the Red Queen asks Alice how bread is made. Alice responds that you begin with flour, only to be interrupted by the queen asking, "Where do you pick the flower?" Other homonym mix-ups add to the confusion. (Lewis Carroll was famous for playing with words and even invented a number of word games.)

Examples to Share

hoarse/horse	hoes/hose	heard/herd
hay/hey	hour/our	new/knew
piece/peace	roll/role	shoe/shoo
whale/wail	doe/dough	pane/pain
hi/high	I'll/aisle	main/mane
peek/peak	raise/rays	ant/aunt
flea/flee	days/daze	knight/night
higher/hire	in/inn	oar/or
chilly/chili	right/write	tide/tied
toe/tow	toad/towed	too/two
whole/hole	cheap/cheep	which/witch
moose/mousse	weak/week	know/no

Ways to Play

◆ Pick a Pear of Pairs: Create an inter-active tabletop "Pear (Pair) Tree" display that will allow children to play with homonyms. To make the tree and play the game, just follow these directions:

1. Stick a tree branch in a lump of clay, then place it in an empty coffee can or flower pot.

2. Pour marbles or pebbles over the clay to help stabilize and secure the branch.

3. Reproducible page 26 includes pear patterns with homonyms written on them. Cut out each pear shape, punch a hole through the top, and attach a loop of string. Hang the pears on the tree.

4. Invite children to take turns trying to find and pick homonym pairs/pears from the tree.

On page 27 you'll find patterns for blank pears. Make a few photocopies of this page, then cut out the shapes and put them in a basket near your pear/pair tree. Invite children to begin looking for homonyms in their spelling words and books they read. Children can record the homonyms on the blank pear shapes and add them to the tree for an ongoing display.

Homonym Resources

A Chocolate Moose for Dinner by F. Gwynne (Windmill, 1976).

The Dove Dove by M. Terban (Clarion, 1988).

Eight Ate: A Feast of Homonym Riddles by M. Terban (Clarion, 1982).

Homophone Riddles to Boost Your Word Power! by G. Maestro (Clarion, 1986).

The King Who Rained by F. Gwynne (Windmill Books, 1970).

What's a Frank Frank? by G. Maestro (Clarion, 1984).

What's a Mite Might? by G. Maestro (Clarion, 1986).

Pear Patterns

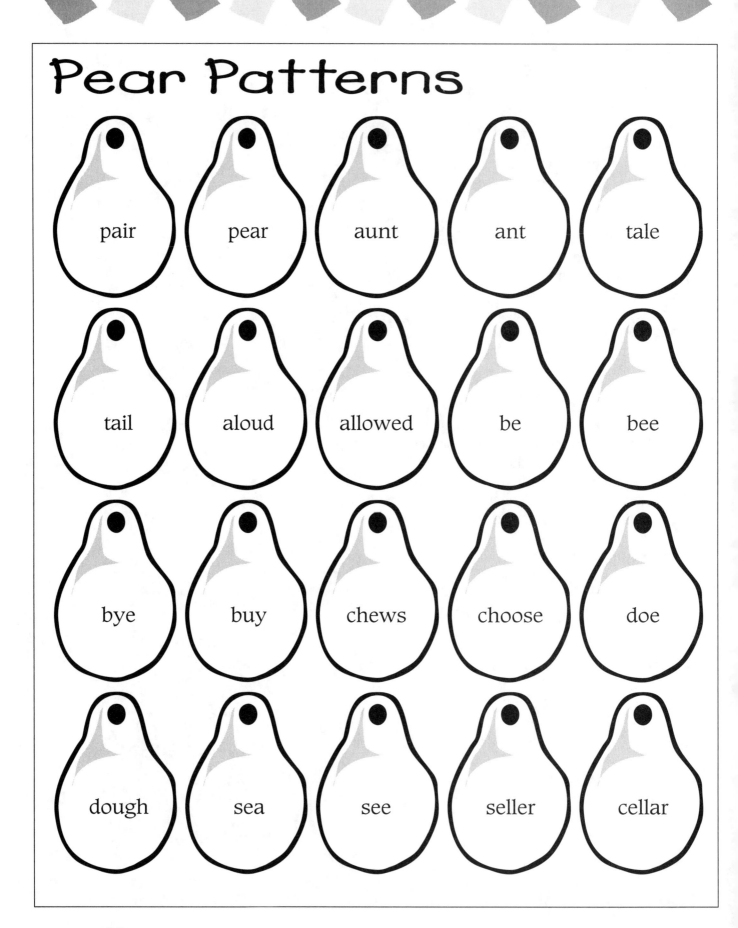

pair   pear   aunt   ant   tale

tail   aloud   allowed   be   bee

bye   buy   chews   choose   doe

dough   sea   see   seller   cellar

Pear Patterns

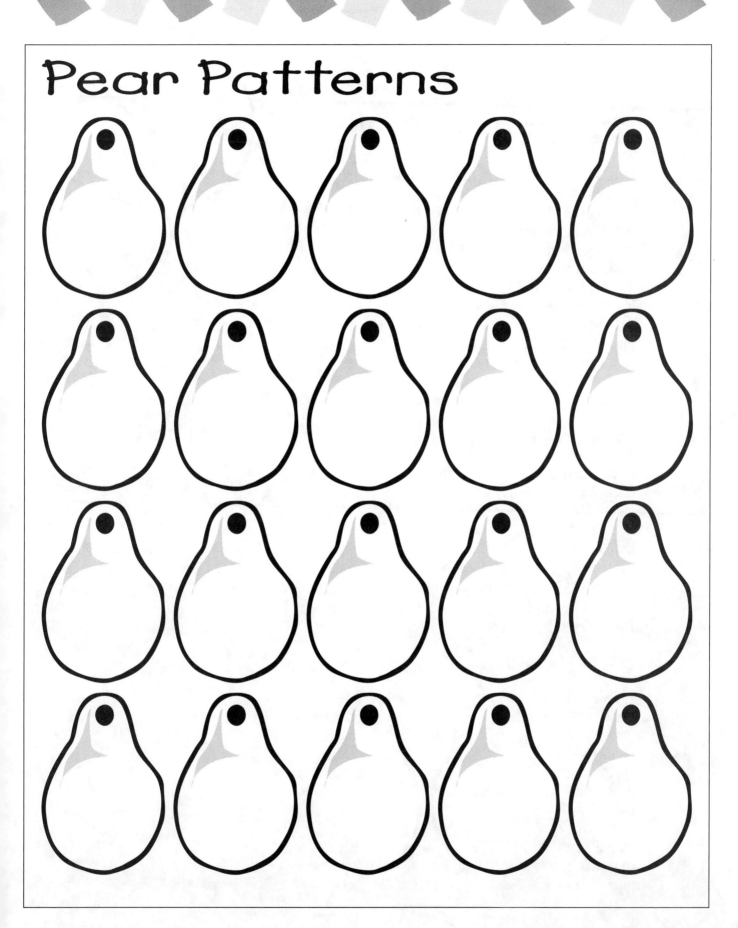

Synonyms

What's a Synonym?

A synonym is a word that has the same or almost the same meaning as another word.

Introducing Synonyms to Kids

Explain synonyms to students by playing the "Great Game," in which the whole class makes a game out of coming up with synonyms for praising student work. After defining what a synonym is, you might say something like: "Today we're going to try to use as many synonyms as we can that mean 'great.' I'll think of as many as I can, and you can help me." Then, every time you praise a student, call attention to the fact that you are using a synonym for "great," such as "excellent," "fine," "terrific," and so on (see other synonyms for "great" listed below). Pretend to get stumped once in a while, and ask for volunteers to help you.

Extend this practice to other parts of your day whenever possible, for example, in describing the weather ("hot, warm, roasting," etc. or "cold, icy, chilly," etc.), a story ("scary, frightening, spooky," etc.), or a snack ("good, delicious, yummy," etc.).

Examples to Share

Synonyms for "great":

excellent	fine
terrific	outstanding
amazing	stellar
fabulous	wonderful
spectacular	stupendous
sensational	well done
swell	awesome
splendid	super
magnificent	first-rate
tremendous	superb
marvelous	

Ways to Play

❥ **Spin-O-Nyms:** Kids can play an easy and fun spinner game to practice coming up with synonyms. "Spin-O-Nyms" is played just like the "A Rhyme in Time" spinner game (see directions on page 16 for setting up and playing game). Use the spinner pattern on page 30 to play.

❥ **Word Wheels:** Students can brainstorm and share synonyms by making "Word Wheels" to display on the wall. To make the word wheels, write a common word in the center of a white paper plate or circle cut from cardboard. Draw a small circle around the word, and "spokes" radiating out from it. Hang the wheel on the wall, and invite children to write on the spokes synonyms for the word in the center of the wheel (be sure to pick words that will offer a number of possible synonyms). You can hang several wheels featuring different overused words on the wall for an extended period of time. Invite children to add to the wheels as they discover synonyms in their reading and other activities. I create a banner for these word wheels titled "Tired, Overused Words" and keep them on display for children to use as a resource for finding exciting, more descriptive words to use in their own writing.

Synonym Resources

A First Thesaurus by H. Wittels and J. Greisman (Western, 1985).

Spin-O-Nyms

Follow these directions to make the spinner for a game of "Spin-O-Nyms."

What you need:
◆ spinner pattern
◆ oak tag (8" x 10")
◆ glue
◆ scissors
◆ brass fastener
◆ paper clip

What you do:
1. Glue this pattern page onto the oak tag.
2. Cut out the spinner pattern.
3. Open a paper clip to form an **S** shape.
4. Use a brass fastener to attach one end of the open paper clip to the center of the spinner, as shown.

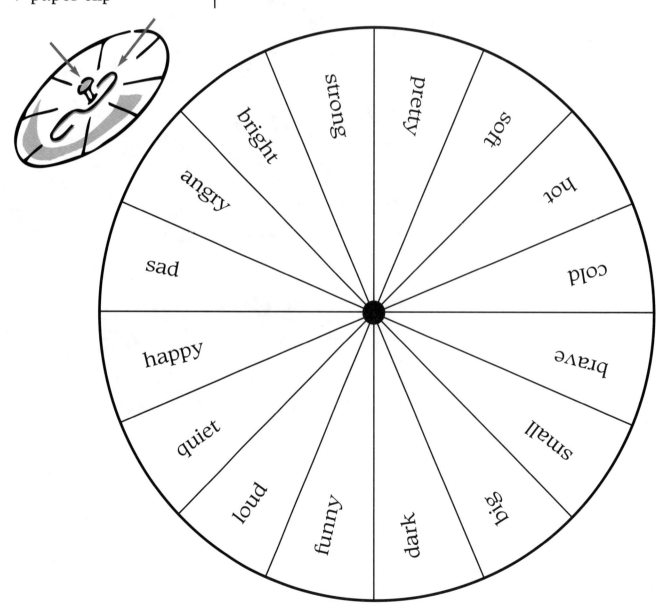

Antonyms

What's an Antonym?
An antonym is a word that is the opposite or near opposite of another word in meaning.

Introducing Antonyms to Kids
After defining what an antonym is, play this quick game to reinforce the concept that antonyms are opposites: Go around the room naming objects or people with a specific characteristic, then ask kids to find and name objects or people with the opposite characteristic. For example: Tom's hair is curly; Juanita's hair is straight; this paper is white; the chalk board is black; this penny is small; this table is big, and so on. As you play the game, record the antonym word pairs on the chalkboard or chart paper.

Examples to Share

day/night	stop/go	high/low
heavy/light	fat/thin	up/down
fast/slow	in/out	short/tall
right/wrong	nice/mean	before/after
enter/exit	big/little	give/take
begin/end	friend/enemy	laugh/cry
over/under	dirty/clean	cheerful/gloomy
sunny/rainy	whisper/scream	rough/smooth

Ways to Play
❥ **Antonym Dominoes:** Children can learn about antonyms by playing a game of dominoes, using the playing pieces on reproducible page 33. To set up and play the game:
1. Divide children into pairs. Provide each pair of students with the Antonym Dominoes page, and tell them to cut out the dominoes. (Note: For added durability, copy page 33 onto cardstock and/or laminate dominoes.)

2. Students should lay the dominoes face down on a tabletop or the floor. Have children swirl the dominoes around to mix them up.

3. Each child should take six dominoes and lay them faceup. They should take another domino and lay it faceup between them. The remaining dominoes should be kept facedown in a nearby pile.

4. Determine who goes first by a coin toss. The first player should then look at his or her dominoes to see if he or she has a domino that contains an antoymn for one of the words on the domino in the center of play. If yes, the child can lay the domino next to its antonym (positioning it either horizontally or vertically). If no, the child should pick a domino from the shared pile.

5. Play proceeds in this way, with children taking turns. The winner is the first person to be rid of all his or her dominoes. Occasionaly, a situation may arise in which neither player can make a match, because the dominoes needed are all in play. In this instance, the winner is the player with the fewest dominoes left.

Children may want to make their own dominoes to add to the pool of playing pieces.

❥ Pick a Pair of Opposites: Adapt the pair/pear tree display described on page 25 to allow kids to "Pick a Pair of Opposites." Antonyms can be written on any desired shape and hung from the tree. Children can then try to pick two shapes that contain words that are opposite in meaning. Encourage children to come up with antonym pairs to add to the tree.

Antonym Resources

Big and Little by J. Mumford (Grosset, 1977).
Big and Little: A Book of Opposites by R. Scarry (Golden, 1986).
Demi's Opposites: An Animal Game Book by Demi (Grosset, 1987).
John Birningham's Opposites by J. Birningham (Crown, 1986).

Antonym Dominoes

cold/big	sweet/hot	little/happy
quiet/wet	sweet/bad	asleep/good
cold/loud	play/black	white/asleep
awake/wet	awake/play	near/work
far/young	loud/happy	sad/near
old/big	far/black	dry/hot
young/sour	white/old	sad/little
quiet/dry	good/work	sour/bad

Chapter 3

Playing with Structure

Palindromes

What's a Palindrome?
A palindrome is a word, phrase, or sentence which reads the same backward or forward.

Introducing Palindromes to Kids
On the chalkboard or overhead projector, draw a picture of a make-believe family which includes a mother, father, and little girl. Challenge children to think of a three-letter word to name each family member. Tell them that each word should begin and end with the same letter. If students get stuck, you may want to offer them clues, for example, "What's another name for mother that rhymes with the name Tom?"

Once each family member has been given a three-letter name ("mom"; "dad" or "pop"; "sis" or "tot"), ask children to spell the words backward and forward. What do they notice? Tell students that words and sentences that can be read the same backward and forward are called palindromes. Share some more examples from the list on page 35. For young children, you may want to limit your lesson to palindromic words; older students may be up to the challenge of palindromic phrases and sentences.

Examples to Share

Words:

I	tot
a	dud
Mom	sees
Dad	radar
pop	Anna
noon	deed
level	toot
Otto	eye
eve	nun
peep	mum
pep	wow
ewe	madam
did	hah
kayak	ma'am
Bob	bib

Phrases and Sentences:

no lemon, no melon
snip pins
May a Pop pop a yam?
Sleep on no peels!
Able was I ere I saw Elba.
Rats live on no evil star.

Ways to Play

❥ **Pick a Palindrome:** Reproducible page 37 is designed to give students some independent practice with palindromes. Once they're familiar with palindromes, encourage students to look for them in literature. They can also look for palindromic numbers in math (such as 22, 101, 737, and so on). Students can record palindromes they find on simple flower shapes cut from colored paper. Use the flowers to make a garden bulletin-board display announcing "Palindromes Are Popping Up All Over."

❥ **Who Said That?:** On reproducible page 38, you'll find a drawing activity that focuses on onomatopoeic palindromes. You may want to review onomatopoeia with your class before distributing a copy of the page to each child.

❥ **Silly Sentences:** More advanced students may enjoy reading and even trying to create palindromic phrases or sentences, which, like palindromic words, read the same backward and forward. Students can use as models some of the phrases and sentences included in the "Examples to Share" section above. Provide children with a list of palindromic words and palindromic helpers (see list below) to use as resources. Palindrome helpers, also known as reversals, are words that form different words when written backwards. For example, the word "net" becomes "ten". These words can be combined with palindromic words to create palindromic sentences. Remind children that their sentences can be silly, and tell them not to get frustrated—writing palindromic sentences is quite difficult even for masters of wordplay.

Palindrome Helpers:

but	no	not
saw	yam	mood
live	now	keep
net	draw	leg
strap	tar	top
stop	star	team
spat	span	step
reward	cod	slap

Palindrome Resources

Go Hang a Salami! I'm a Lasagna Hog! and Other Palindromes by J. Agee (Farrar, Straus and Giroux, 1991).

Teapot, Switcheroo, and Other Silly Word Games by R. Tremain (Greenwillow Books, 1979).

Too Hot to Hoot, Funny Palindrome Riddles by M. Terban (Clarion, 1985).

Name _____

Pick a Palindrome

Can you guess the palindrome that answers each question?
Use the word box to help you. Write the palindrome on the line next to
the question it answers.

Palindrome Word Box

eye	Bob	dud
pup	pep	noon
bib	tot	

1. What do you call something that's a flop? _____

2. What's a short name for Robert? _____

3. What's a baby dog? _____

4. What do you have if you have lots of energy? _____

5. What does a baby wear to keep food off her clothes? _____

6. What's a small child? _____

7. What helps you see? _____

8. What's another way to say 12 o' clock? _____

More! Can you think of other palindromes? Make up a question that has a
palindrome as an answer. Ask your friend the question. See if your friend
can guess the palindrome answer.

Name _____

Who Said That?

The speech balloons below have sound words in them. Each of the sound words is a palindrome. Draw a picture of an animal, person, or thing that makes each palindrome sound.

More! The answer to this riddle is a palindrome. Can you guess what it is?

How did the owl feel on the first day of summer?

(Turn page upside down for the answer.)

Anagrams

What's an Anagram?
An anagram is a word or phrase made by switching the letters around in another word or phrase.

Introducing Anagrams to Kids
Anagrams can be a bit challenging for young kids who are still learning to recognize letter patterns, but they're quite useful in helping students develop spelling skills and build vocabulary. A good way to introduce anagrams to students is to let them actually manipulate the letters of different words. Provide students with individual letter manipulatives (plastic pieces, paper cut-outs, or even alphabet cereal can be used). Tell children to use the letter manipulatives to spell the word "lump." Then ask them if they can turn the word "lump" into a piece of fruit by rearranging it's letters. Explain that the new word "plum," made by switching around the letters of the word "lump," is called an anagram.

Examples to Share

pest = step	tools = stool
lump = plum	odor = door
spot = stop	march = charm
slip = lips	stove = votes
snow = owns	mane = name
pea = ape	tale = late
grab = brag	two = tow
rat = art	tower = wrote
went = newt	town = won't

Ways to Play
➤ **Letter Switcheroo:** Reproducible page 41 includes some simple anagram riddles for children to solve. If kids get stuck on a word, tell them to look at the picture-border for clues to the answers.

➤ **Anagram Lace-Up Pattern:** Use the pattern on page 42 to make a "lace-up" card to give kids practice with anagrams. Here's what you do:
1. Make a photocopy of the pattern page.
2. Glue the pattern page to an empty file folder.
3. Cut out the front and back patterns and glue them together, with print facing out on each side. Be sure that the arrows on the front and back of the card both point up, so that the patterns are properly matched.
4. Use a hole-punch or pencil point to make a hole in the upper-left-hand corner, where indicated.
5. Cut a six-foot piece of string or yarn and loop it through the hole. Knot the end of the string to tie it to the card.

To use the lace-up, kids should pull the string into the notch next to the word "limes" in the upper-left-hand corner of the card. They should then run the string to an anagram match for "limes" on the right-hand side of the card, wrapping the string behind the notch and back up to the second word in the left-hand column ("wasp"). Children should continue to wrap the string in this back-and-forth manner until they have found an anagram match for each word.

Tell children to be sure to wrap the string for the last pair of words twice, so that the string runs across the front and back of the card. Students can check if they've made the right matches by flipping the card over. The string should follow the lines on the answer key. If it doesn't, have kids unwrap the string and try to make the matches again.

❥ Edible Anagrams: Tiny alphabet-shaped cookie cutters are available from many baking supply stores. Enlist student's help to bake up several batches of letters using a simple sugar-cookie or gingerbread recipe. Students will have lots of fun making—and eating—their own words as they manipulate the letters to make anagrams. Be sure students record their anagrams on a class word list before consuming them!

❥ Heads or Tails?: Here are two more quick games that involve playing with letters:
- *Beheadment*: Challenge kids to find words that form new words when their first letter is dropped, (e.g., "plate" becomes "late"; "when" becomes "hen"; "train" becomes "rain").
- *Curtailment:* Challenge kids to find words that form new words when their last letter is dropped, (e.g., "time" becomes "Tim"; "wind" becomes "win"; "song" becomes "son")

Anagram Resources
Alphabake: A Cookbook and Cookie Cutter Set by D. Pearson, (Dutton, 1995).

Name _____

Letter Switcheroo

Try to answer the questions below. To find the answer, switch around the letters of each underlined word. You'll find clues to the answers in the pictures scattered around this page.

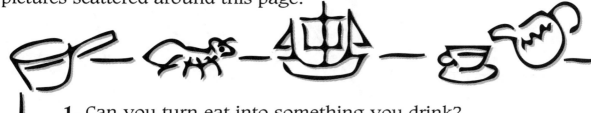

1. Can you turn <u>eat</u> into something you drink?
_____

2. Can you turn the color <u>tan</u> into a bug? _____

3. Can you turn <u>sore</u> into a sweet-smelling flower?
_____

4. Can you turn <u>hips</u> into something that sails the seas?
_____

5. Can you turn <u>snoop</u> into something you eat with?
_____

6. Can you turn <u>shore</u> into a galloping animal?
_____

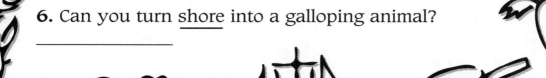

More! The word *spot* is an anagram for two other words. Can you come up with both of them?

Anagram Lace-Up Pattern

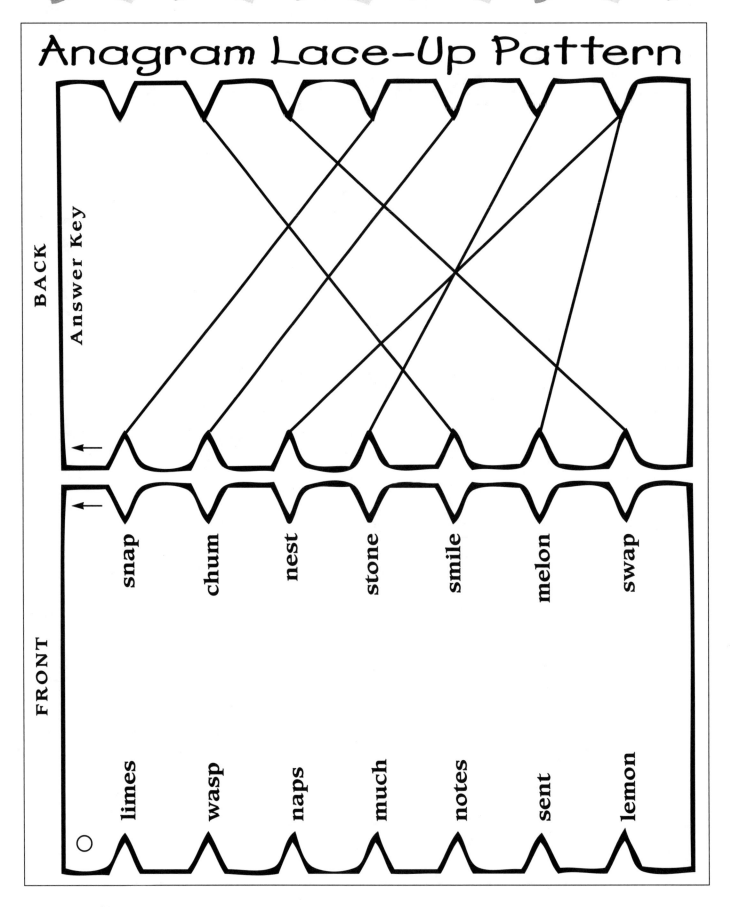

BACK

Answer Key

FRONT

snap

chum

nest

stone

smile

melon

swap

limes

wasp

naps

much

notes

sent

lemon

Sillies

What's a Silly?

A sillie is a game that involves playing with the last syllable of a multi-syllable word. The last syllable must be able to stand on its own as a separate word. The word formed by the last syllable must also have multiple meanings. For example, the last syllable of the word "elbow" is "bow," which has a number of definitions. To make a sillie, you create a series of "silly" definitions for the single- and multi-syllable words that follow this pattern:

There's a *bow* you put on a package.
There's a *bow* that plays a violin.
But a *bow* that's found on your arm is an _____bow.

(answer: elbow)

Introducing Sillies to Kids

Begin by making sure students understand what a syllable is. Write a list of multi-syllable words on the board that end with a single-syllable word, such as: rainbow, island, pilot, toucan, hurricane, and so on. Ask kids what they notice about the last syllable of these words. Once you've established that the last syllable forms a separate word, point out that these words also have more than one meaning. Ask students to write or dictate sentences that demonstrate the different meanings of the word.

Tell kids you're going to introduce them to a game using words like these. Then write a few sillies from the list below on the chalkboard or a spiral chart. (I like writing sillies on charts because it's easy to stand them on the chalk ledge for all to see. Then the charts can be reused from year to year.) Walk kids through the game till they get the hang of it. Sillies are fun to solve and fun to create, but they're also a little tricky. You'll want to give kids lots of teacher-guided practice before they try to solve them independently or make their own sillies.

Examples to Share

There's a *key* that means the main one.
There's a *key* that's an island.
But a *key* that eats bananas is a _____key.

(answer: monkey)

There's a *ball* that you throw or bounce.
There's a *ball* that's a big party with dancing.
But a *ball* you can eat is a _____ball.

(answer: meatball)

There's a *pet* that can be a dog or a cat.
There's a *pet* that means to stroke softly.
But a *pet* that covers a floor is a _____pet.

(answer: carpet)

More Silly Samples

Depending on the age and ability level of your students, you can loosen the rules somewhat for creating sillies. Following are two examples of sillies that use a multi-syllable word whose last syllable suggests a word in sound, but isn't actually a word on its own. The last one is a silly that uses a real word ("no").

There's a *doe* that's a female deer.
There's a *dough* that's unbaked bread.
But a *dow* you can see through is a _____dow.

(answer: window)

There's a *row* that means a line of people or things.
There's a *row* that means to paddle through the water.
But a *ro* that's a person who has done something brave is a _____ro.

(answer: hero)

There's a *no* that's the opposite of yes.
There's a *know* that means to understand.
But a *no* that has keys and is played to make music is a _____no.

(answer: piano)

Ways to Play

❧ **Solve a Silly:** Distribute a copy of reproducible page 46 to each child. Older students may be able to figure out the sillies on their own, but you may want to allow younger children to work in pairs or teams to solve them. Follow up by showing kids how they can make their own sillies. Show students how to scan a page in the dictionary looking for words that have more than one syllable. They should then check to see if the last syllable could be a word on its own. If this word has at least two meanings, voila!, they have a silly! Create your own silly "dictionary" of sillies that kids can add to as they invent new ones.

❥ Sillies can be used with older students as an enrichment to thematic study. For example, in a study of U.S. geography, you could have students create sillies using the names of cities or states, as in the following examples:

There's a *sea* that means ocean.
There's a *see* that means to view with your eyes.
But a *see* in the southern United States is _____see.

(answer: Tennessee)

There's a *son* that's the opposite of daughter.
There's a *sun* that gives us light.
But a *son* that's the capital of Wisconsin is _____son.

(answer: Madison)

Silly Resource
The dictionary is your best friend for creating sillies!

Name _____

Solve a Silly

Can you figure out the answers to these sillies? Cut out the pictures at the bottom of the page. Glue each picture in a box next to the silly it answers. The first one is done for you.

1. There's a *room* that means space.
   There's a *room* that means a part of a house.
   But a *room* you can eat is a _____room.

   _____

2. There's a *bow* that you can wear in your hair.
   There's a *bow* that goes with an arrow.
   But a *bow* of beautiful colors in the sky is a _____bow.

   _____

3. There's a *key* that fits a lock.
   There's a *key* that you find on a piano.
   But a *key* that has feathers is a _____key.

   _____

4. There's a *low* that is the opposite of high.
   There's a *low* that means feeling sad.
   But a *low* you can sleep on is a _____low.

   _____

5. There's a *den* that's a room in a house.
   There's a *den* where bears live.
   But a *den* where flowers grow is a _____den.

   _____

6. There's a ball that means a good time.
   There's a ball that you play with.
   But a ball you can chew and blow bubbles with is a _____ball.

More! Try to write a silly using one of these words: fall, fit, land, saw.

Chapter 4

Playing with Picture and Word Puzzles

Puniddles

What's a Puniddle?

A puniddle is a type of puzzle in which two pictures are combined to suggest a word with a separate meaning. These picture riddles are often shown in a funny or "punny" way, hence the name. A puniddle may have a compound word as its solution. For example pictures of a tooth and a brush would suggest the word "toothbrush." Or, the pictures may suggest a word in sound only, for example, pictures of a cornfield and a knee would suggest the word "corny."

Introducing Puniddles to Kids

Use Bruce and Brett McMillan's book *Puniddles* to show students how these picture riddles work. The McMillans use two photographs to represent a word: a cow next to a group of boys represents the word "cowboys"; a campfire next to a cracker represents the word "firecracker," and so on. If the McMillans' book is unavailable, try drawing some puniddles on an overhead projector transparency to introduce kids to this game (see examples that follow).

Examples to Share

+ = catfish

 = toadstool

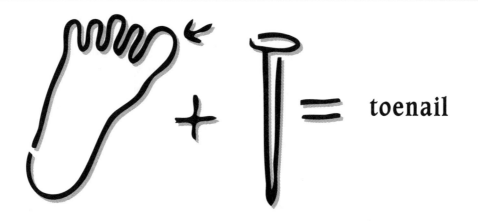 = toenail

 = earring

 = crabby

= pantry

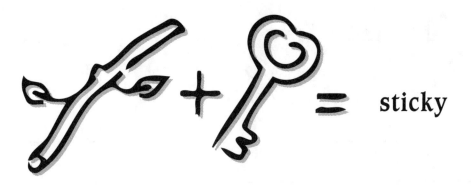

= sticky

Ways to Play

❥ **Very Punny!:** Reproducible page 50 includes puniddles for kids to solve. Some of the puniddles in this activity make compound words; others just suggest a word in sound. After kids have solved the puniddles, ask them to determine which answers are compound words.

❥ **Picture Pairs:** Puniddles lend themselves naturally to a study of compound words. Reproducible page 51 includes pictures kids can use to create puniddles that form compound words. Divide children into pairs, and provide them with a copy of the picture page. After they have cut apart the pictures, allow children to take turns putting the pictures together to make puniddles for their partners to solve. (Many of the pictures can be paired in a variety of ways, such as butterfly and buttercup, bookbag and handbag, and so on). Encourage partners to record all the compound words they come up with, then compare their word list with those of other teams. Can students think of other compound words that might be illustrated with pairs of pictures? Encourage them to draw their own picture squares to add to the game.

❥ **Puniddle Picture Hunt:** Another way for kids to make puniddles is to hunt through magazines for pairs of pictures that suggest new words. Students can paste each pair of pictures on one side of a blank index card, then write the answer to the puniddle on the other. Store the puniddle cards in a basket for free-time fun.

Puniddle Resource
Puniddles by Bruce McMillan and Brett McMillan (Houghton Mifflin, 1982).

Name _____

Very Punny!

Each pair of pictures stands for a word. Can you figure out what it is?
Cut out the pictures at the bottom of the page. Paste each picture in the box
next to the puniddle it answers.

eyeglasses   pineapple   starfish   penny

More! On the back of this paper, draw pictures to make puniddles for the
words below:

cowgirl   treetop   seasaw

Picture Pairs

Rebuses

What's a Rebus?
A rebus is a visual puzzle in which a word, phrase, or sentence is represented by pictures, letters, numbers, and symbols. A rebus must be read aloud to be solved.

Introducing Rebuses to Kids
Children love rebuses, and they can be adapted for all ability levels. Begin by introducing kids to simple rebuses for words or phrases, then move on to complete sentences. (Puniddles are actually a good introduction to rebuses, since they give kids practice in associating picture clues with words.) Show students how to decipher a rebus by saying the names of the pictures and letters out loud; explain that "+" and "-" signs mean that a sound should be added or subtracted.

I like to draw rebuses on large spiral charts so they can be reused, but rebuses can also be quickly sketched on a chalkboard. Rebus sketches can be as simple as stick figures. You may want to enlist the help of children who like to draw to make the rebus puzzles. Sound out a few puzzles together. Sometimes I give kids a hint if the rebus is particularly challenging rebus or if they seem stumped.

Examples to Share

Words and Phrases:

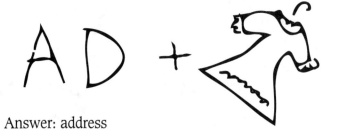

Answer: address

Answer: candy cane

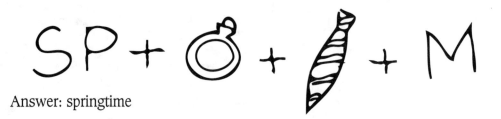

Answer: springtime

Answer: too late

Answer: be polite

Sentences:

Answer: I love you!

U + R + A + ☆

Answer: You are a star.

Answer: I can see you.

Answer: Be nice to mice.

Here is a rebus that Sallie, a second grader, wrote to me in her dialogue journal. It says, "I love my book club book!":

Ways to Play

➤ **Good Enough to Eat!** Once you've walked kids through some rebus puzzles, distribute reproducible page 55 for independent work. As a follow-up to this rebus activity focusing on food, encourage children to come up with rebuses for other edible items. Then compile their ideas on an oversized, illustrated menu made from posterboard.

➤ **At the Zoo:** Challenge students to make rebuses for different kinds of animals. Children can ask classmates to try to solve their animal rebuses. You might want to write the following rebus on the chalkboard for students to use as a model:

Answer: elephant

➤ **Once Upon a Rebus:** Invite children to work in small groups to create simple rebus retellings of familiar fairy tales, such as "Goldilocks and the Three Bears" or "The Three Little Pigs." They can substitute pictures of people, animals, houses, and objects for some of the words in the story. You may want to provide children with some of the rebus storybooks below to use as models in creating their rebus rewrites.

Rebus Resources
Bunny Rabbit Rebus by D. Adler (Crowell, 1983).
From A to Z: The Collected Letters of Irene and Hallie Coletta by I. Coletta (Prentice-Hall, 1979).
Happy Hanukkah Rebus by D. Adler (Viking, 1989).
Happy Thanksgiving Rebus by D. Adler (Viking, 1991).

Good Enough to Eat!

What's on the menu? It's hard to tell because it's written in rebus!
Try to solve the rebuses to figure out what each food is. Write the answer to
each rebus on the back of this page.

More! Can you make up a rebus for another kind of food? Draw your rebus on
the back of this paper. Give it to a friend to solve.

Answers

Noisy Words, page 14: Children should match the pictures with these words: drum, ratta-tat-tat; mouse, squeak; car, beep-beep; tennis racket, whack; clock, tick-tick-tick; cymbals, crash.

Get Ready to Rhyme, page 17: The missing rhyming words should be filled in in the following order: door, icicle, cat, whale, goat, skyscraper, sight.

Ready, Set, Rhyme, page 21: Check students' work to see that they made the following matches:

What's an angry father? .... mad dad

What's a flower that
doesn't want to work? .... lazy daisy

What's something on the
stove that you
shouldn't touch? .... hot pot

What's a song sung in
the summer? .... June tune

What's a wet light? .... damp lamp

What's a noisy
group of people? .... loud croud

Pick a Palindrome, page 37: 1. dud, 2. Bob, 3. pup, 4. pep, 5. bib, 6. tot, 7. eye, 8. noon.

Who Said That?, page 38: Children's drawings may vary, but following are four possible ways to illustrate the palindromes included: "toot," horn; "peep," chick; "pop," balloon being pricked with a pin; "hah," person laughing.

Letter Switcheroo, page 41: 1. tea, 2. ant, 3. rose, 4. ship, 5. spoon, 6. horse. More! pots and tops.

Solve a Silly, page 46: 1. mushroom, 2. rainbow, 3. turkey, 4. pillow, 5. garden, 6. gumball.

Very Punny, page 50: Children should paste pictures of the following in the boxes: 1. starfish, 2. pineapple, 3. penny, 4. eyeglasses.

Picture Pairs, page 51: Following is a list of the possible compound words children may form using the pictures: handball, football, fireball, snowball, handbook, handbag, buttercup, butterfly, butterball, cupcake, pancake, footman, horseman, fireman, snowman, horseshoe, horsefly, firefly, snowshoe.

Good Enough to Eat, page 55: 1. radishes, 2. potatoes, 3. apple sauce, 4. cherry pie.